The Littlest Clown

written by Jay Dale

illustrated by Mélanie Florian

Clancy Brown was a little clown.
He had fuzzy orange hair
and a big red nose.
He could run around,
and jump up and down.

Clancy Brown was the littlest clown
at the Tip Top Circus.

Clancy's mum and dad
were clowns, too.
Mrs Brown had short red hair
and a funny green nose.
Mr Brown had big purple pants
and long blue shoes.

The Browns were the best clowns
at the Tip Top Circus.

But one day, Clancy stopped.
He did not run around,
and he did not jump up and down.
Clancy looked sad.

"Whatever is the matter, Clancy?"
asked Mrs Brown, after the show.
"Why do you look so sad?"

Big tears ran down Clancy's face.
"I don't want to be a clown,"
he said.
"I want to be a fireman.
I want to ride in a big red truck
and put on a fireman's hat."

"Oh, dear," said Mr Brown.
"Whatever will we do?
We need a little clown to run around,
and to jump up and down."

"Well," said Clancy,

"I don't want to be a clown.

I want to be a fireman."

Mrs Brown looked at Mr Brown.

Then she looked at Clancy.

"Well," she said,

"I don't want to be a clown.

I want to be a doctor

and help sick people."

"Well," said Mr Brown,
"I don't want to be a clown.
I want to be a farmer
and grow lots of carrots."

So the very next day,
Clancy Brown and his mum
and dad left the circus.
They went a long way away,
and they did not come back.

Now Clancy is a fireman,
Mrs Brown is a doctor
and Mr Brown is a farmer.
And everyone is happy!